EMMANUEL JOSEPH

Tech Pulse: Life in the Fast Lane of Innovation

Copyright © 2025 by Emmanuel Joseph

All rights reserved. No part of this publication may be reproduced, stored or transmitted in any form or by any means, electronic, mechanical, photocopying, recording, scanning, or otherwise without written permission from the publisher. It is illegal to copy this book, post it to a website, or distribute it by any other means without permission.

First edition

This book was professionally typeset on Reedsy.
Find out more at reedsy.com

Contents

1	Chapter 1: The Dawn of Innovation	1
2	Chapter 2: The Digital Revolution	3
3	Chapter 3: Rise of Artificial Intelligence	5
4	Chapter 4: The Internet of Things	7
5	Chapter 5: Blockchain and Cryptocurrencies	9
6	Chapter 6: The Impact of Social Media	11
7	Chapter 7: The Future of Work	13
8	Chapter 8: Sustainable Technology	15
9	Chapter 9: Biotechnology and Health	18
10	Chapter 10: The Role of Education	20
11	Chapter 11: The Ethics of Innovation	22
12	Chapter 12: Looking to the Future	24

1

Chapter 1: The Dawn of Innovation

In the beginning, innovation was a spark that ignited human curiosity. It started with simple tools fashioned from stone and wood. These early inventions laid the groundwork for a future where human ingenuity knew no bounds. As societies evolved, so did their technologies, transforming the way people lived, worked, and connected with one another.

The agricultural revolution was a pivotal moment in history. With the advent of farming tools and techniques, humanity was able to settle in one place, cultivating crops and domesticating animals. This shift from nomadic lifestyles to settled communities allowed for population growth and the establishment of complex societies. Innovations in agriculture not only provided sustenance but also paved the way for other technological advancements.

Fast forward to the industrial revolution, a period that saw unprecedented technological progress. Steam engines, mechanized looms, and the telegraph revolutionized industries and communication. Factories became the heart of economic growth, producing goods at a scale never seen before. This era of innovation transformed the global landscape, ushering in modern urbanization and the rise of industrialized nations.

As we entered the 20th century, the pace of innovation accelerated. The invention of the automobile, the telephone, and electricity fundamentally changed daily life. These technologies shrank distances and connected people like never before. The world was becoming a smaller, more interconnected place, setting the stage for the digital revolution that would follow.

The digital age began with the invention of computers and the internet. These innovations revolutionized how we process and share information. The rise of personal computers in the 1980s and the internet in the 1990s brought about a new era of connectivity and communication. People could now access vast amounts of information at their fingertips, transforming education, business, and entertainment.

In the 21st century, innovation continues to shape our world in ways we could have never imagined. Artificial intelligence, biotechnology, and renewable energy are just a few areas where groundbreaking advancements are occurring. The pace of innovation shows no signs of slowing down, promising a future where technology will continue to redefine the boundaries of possibility.

2

Chapter 2: The Digital Revolution

The digital revolution marked a profound shift in human history. It began with the development of early computers, massive machines that filled entire rooms but performed basic calculations. These early computers laid the foundation for the digital age, setting the stage for smaller, more powerful devices that would transform every aspect of life.

The invention of the microprocessor in the 1970s was a game-changer. This tiny chip, capable of processing vast amounts of data, led to the development of personal computers. Companies like Apple and IBM brought these devices into homes and offices, making computing accessible to the masses. The personal computer revolutionized industries, from finance to education, and changed how people worked and communicated.

The internet, initially developed as a military communication network, quickly became a global phenomenon. In the 1990s, the World Wide Web emerged, allowing people to access information and connect with others across the globe. Websites, email, and online forums transformed how we share and consume information. The internet democratized knowledge, making it available to anyone with an internet connection.

Social media platforms emerged in the 2000s, changing how we interact and share our lives. Sites like Facebook, Twitter, and Instagram became virtual spaces where people could connect, share, and engage with one another. Social media gave rise to new forms of communication, from memes to viral videos, and created opportunities for influencers and content creators to reach global audiences.

The rise of smartphones further accelerated the digital revolution. These pocket-sized devices combined the power of a computer with the connectivity of the internet. Apps revolutionized how we perform everyday tasks, from banking to navigation. Smartphones became essential tools, enabling us to stay connected, informed, and entertained wherever we go.

As we move deeper into the digital age, emerging technologies like artificial intelligence, blockchain, and the Internet of Things are pushing the boundaries of innovation. AI is transforming industries with applications in healthcare, finance, and transportation. Blockchain is revolutionizing how we handle transactions and data security. The Internet of Things is creating a connected world where everyday objects communicate and collaborate.

The digital revolution has profoundly changed how we live, work, and interact. It has created new opportunities and challenges, reshaping societies and economies. As we continue to innovate and push the boundaries of technology, the digital revolution promises to shape the future in ways we can only begin to imagine.

3

Chapter 3: Rise of Artificial Intelligence

Artificial Intelligence (AI) represents one of the most significant technological advancements of our time. It began with early attempts to create machines that could mimic human intelligence. The concept of AI dates back to ancient myths and legends of automatons, but it wasn't until the 20th century that real progress was made.

In the mid-20th century, researchers began developing algorithms and computer programs that could perform tasks requiring human intelligence. These early AI systems were limited in scope, often designed for specific tasks like playing chess or solving mathematical problems. However, they laid the groundwork for more advanced AI systems that would emerge in the following decades.

The advent of machine learning in the 1980s and 1990s was a turning point for AI. Machine learning algorithms enabled computers to learn from data and improve their performance over time. This approach allowed AI systems to tackle more complex problems, from image recognition to natural language processing. The rise of big data in the 21st century provided AI with vast amounts of information to learn from, further accelerating its development.

AI has made significant strides in various fields, transforming industries and creating new possibilities. In healthcare, AI is being used to analyze medical data, assist in diagnostics, and develop personalized treatment plans. In finance, AI algorithms are optimizing investment strategies, detecting fraud, and automating trading. In transportation, self-driving cars and drones are revolutionizing how we move goods and people.

One of the most exciting developments in AI is the rise of deep learning. Deep learning algorithms, inspired by the structure of the human brain, have achieved remarkable success in tasks like image and speech recognition. These algorithms can process vast amounts of data and identify patterns that were previously impossible for machines to detect. Deep learning has enabled breakthroughs in fields like computer vision, natural language understanding, and robotics.

Despite its many achievements, AI also raises important ethical and societal questions. As AI systems become more capable, concerns about job displacement, privacy, and bias have emerged. Ensuring that AI is developed and deployed responsibly is a critical challenge for the future. Policymakers, researchers, and industry leaders must work together to create guidelines and regulations that promote the ethical use of AI.

The rise of AI represents a new era of innovation, one that promises to reshape our world in profound ways. As we continue to explore the potential of AI, we must also consider its implications and strive to harness its power for the greater good. The future of AI is bright, and its impact on society will be felt for generations to come.

4

Chapter 4: The Internet of Things

The Internet of Things (IoT) is revolutionizing how we interact with the world around us. IoT refers to a network of interconnected devices, from everyday objects like refrigerators and thermostats to industrial machines and smart cities. These devices communicate and share data, creating a connected ecosystem that enhances our lives in countless ways.

The concept of IoT dates back to the early days of computing, but it wasn't until the advent of the internet and wireless communication that it became a reality. The proliferation of sensors, microcontrollers, and wireless networks has enabled the development of smart devices that can collect, process, and transmit data. IoT has transformed how we live, work, and play, creating new opportunities for innovation and efficiency.

One of the most visible applications of IoT is in smart homes. Devices like smart thermostats, security cameras, and voice assistants have become increasingly popular, offering convenience, security, and energy efficiency. These devices can be controlled remotely, learn user preferences, and even communicate with each other to create a seamless living experience. Smart homes are just the beginning of IoT's potential to transform our daily lives.

IoT is also making a significant impact in industries such as manufacturing, agriculture, and healthcare. In manufacturing, IoT-enabled machines can monitor their own performance, predict maintenance needs, and optimize production processes. This approach, known as Industry 4.0, is increasing efficiency and reducing downtime. In agriculture, IoT sensors can monitor soil conditions, weather, and crop health, enabling farmers to make data-driven decisions and improve yields. In healthcare, wearable devices and remote monitoring systems are helping patients manage chronic conditions and providing doctors with real-time data for better diagnostics and treatment.

Smart cities are another exciting application of IoT. By integrating IoT technology into urban infrastructure, cities can become more efficient, sustainable, and responsive to the needs of their residents. Smart traffic lights can optimize traffic flow, reducing congestion and emissions. IoT sensors can monitor air quality, waste management, and energy consumption, allowing cities to address environmental challenges and improve the quality of life for their inhabitants. Smart cities represent a vision of the future where technology enhances every aspect of urban living.

Despite its many benefits, IoT also presents challenges related to security and privacy. The vast amount of data generated by IoT devices can be a target for cyberattacks, and ensuring the security of these devices is critical. Additionally, the collection and use of personal data by IoT devices raise concerns about privacy and data protection. Addressing these challenges requires a collaborative effort from industry, policymakers, and consumers to create secure and trustworthy IoT ecosystems.

The Internet of Things is transforming our world, creating new opportunities for innovation and efficiency. As we continue to explore the potential of IoT, we must also address the challenges it presents to ensure a secure and sustainable future. The journey of IoT is just beginning, and its impact on our lives

5

Chapter 5: Blockchain and Cryptocurrencies

Blockchain technology and cryptocurrencies have transformed the landscape of finance and digital transactions. Blockchain, the underlying technology behind cryptocurrencies, is a decentralized and distributed ledger that records transactions across multiple computers. This technology ensures transparency, security, and immutability, making it ideal for various applications beyond just digital currencies.

Bitcoin, introduced in 2009 by an anonymous person or group known as Satoshi Nakamoto, was the first cryptocurrency to utilize blockchain technology. Bitcoin's decentralized nature challenged traditional financial systems, offering a peer-to-peer method of transferring value without intermediaries like banks. This innovation opened the door to a new era of financial technology and digital assets.

As Bitcoin gained popularity, other cryptocurrencies emerged, each with unique features and use cases. Ethereum, introduced in 2015 by Vitalik Buterin, expanded the possibilities of blockchain by enabling smart contracts. These self-executing contracts run on the Ethereum blockchain and automatically enforce the terms and conditions agreed upon by the parties involved. Smart contracts have applications in various fields, including finance, supply chain management, and real estate.

Blockchain technology has the potential to revolutionize industries beyond finance. In supply chain management, blockchain can provide end-to-end transparency, allowing stakeholders to track the journey of products from production to delivery. This transparency helps combat counterfeit goods and ensures the authenticity of products. In healthcare, blockchain can secure patient data and streamline medical records, improving data privacy and accessibility.

Decentralized finance, or DeFi, is another significant development enabled by blockchain technology. DeFi refers to a financial system that operates without traditional intermediaries, using smart contracts on blockchain platforms. DeFi applications include lending and borrowing, decentralized exchanges, and yield farming. These platforms offer financial services that are accessible to anyone with an internet connection, democratizing finance and providing opportunities for financial inclusion.

Despite its many benefits, blockchain technology and cryptocurrencies also face challenges. Regulatory uncertainty, scalability issues, and energy consumption are some of the concerns that need to be addressed. Additionally, the volatility of cryptocurrencies can pose risks to investors and users. As the technology matures, it will be crucial to develop frameworks and solutions that address these challenges while maintaining the core principles of decentralization and security.

Blockchain and cryptocurrencies have the potential to reshape the future of finance and beyond. As we continue to explore and develop this technology, we must balance innovation with responsibility, ensuring that the benefits of blockchain are accessible to all while mitigating the risks. The journey of blockchain is just beginning, and its impact on our world will be profound.

6

Chapter 6: The Impact of Social Media

Social media has revolutionized how we communicate, share information, and connect with others. Platforms like Facebook, Twitter, Instagram, and TikTok have become integral parts of our daily lives, influencing everything from personal relationships to global events. The rise of social media has transformed the way we interact and engage with the world around us.

One of the most significant impacts of social media is its ability to connect people across the globe. Social media platforms enable individuals to maintain relationships with friends and family, regardless of geographical distance. They also provide opportunities to meet new people and build online communities around shared interests and experiences. This connectivity has created a more interconnected world, fostering understanding and collaboration.

Social media has also democratized information and amplified voices that might otherwise go unheard. Platforms like Twitter have become powerful tools for activists, journalists, and ordinary citizens to share their perspectives and raise awareness about important issues. Movements like #BlackLivesMatter and #MeToo gained momentum through social media, highlighting the power of these platforms to drive social change and mobilize communities.

However, social media also comes with its challenges. The spread of misinformation and fake news is a significant concern, as false information can quickly go viral and influence public opinion. Social media algorithms, designed to prioritize engaging content, can create echo chambers where users are exposed to only one perspective. This phenomenon can contribute to polarization and hinder constructive dialogue.

The impact of social media on mental health is another critical issue. While social media can provide a sense of connection, it can also contribute to feelings of loneliness, anxiety, and depression. The pressure to present a curated and idealized version of oneself can lead to comparisons and self-esteem issues. It's essential to find a balance and use social media in a way that promotes well-being and meaningful connections.

Privacy and data security are also significant concerns in the age of social media. Platforms collect vast amounts of personal data, raising questions about how this information is used and protected. High-profile data breaches and scandals, like the Cambridge Analytica case, have highlighted the need for robust privacy protections and transparent data practices.

Despite its challenges, social media continues to evolve and shape our world in profound ways. It has become a powerful tool for communication, activism, and entertainment. As we navigate the complexities of social media, it's essential to use these platforms responsibly and thoughtfully, harnessing their potential for positive impact while addressing the challenges they present.

7

Chapter 7: The Future of Work

The future of work is being shaped by technological advancements, shifting societal expectations, and evolving business models. As we navigate the rapidly changing landscape of work, it's essential to understand the trends and forces driving these changes and their implications for individuals and organizations.

Automation and artificial intelligence are at the forefront of the future of work. AI-powered systems and robots are increasingly performing tasks that were once the domain of humans, from manufacturing and logistics to customer service and data analysis. While automation can increase efficiency and productivity, it also raises concerns about job displacement and the need for reskilling and upskilling the workforce.

Remote work is another significant trend reshaping the future of work. The COVID-19 pandemic accelerated the adoption of remote work, demonstrating that many jobs can be performed outside traditional office settings. Remote work offers flexibility and work-life balance but also presents challenges such as maintaining team cohesion, managing productivity, and addressing the digital divide. As remote and hybrid work models become more prevalent, organizations must adapt to new ways of working and supporting their employees.

The gig economy is also transforming the nature of work. Platforms like Uber, Airbnb, and TaskRabbit have created opportunities for individuals to work on a freelance or on-demand basis. The gig economy offers flexibility and autonomy but also raises questions about job security, benefits, and worker rights. Ensuring fair treatment and protections for gig workers will be crucial as this sector continues to grow.

Lifelong learning and continuous skill development are becoming increasingly important in the future of work. As technology evolves and industries change, workers must continually update their skills to remain relevant and competitive. This shift requires a focus on education and training, with an emphasis on digital literacy, critical thinking, and adaptability. Employers, educational institutions, and policymakers must collaborate to create pathways for lifelong learning and career development.

Diversity, equity, and inclusion (DEI) are critical considerations for the future of work. Organizations are recognizing the importance of creating inclusive workplaces that value diverse perspectives and experiences. DEI initiatives promote innovation, improve employee engagement, and drive better business outcomes. As the workforce becomes more diverse, fostering a culture of inclusion will be essential for attracting and retaining top talent.

The future of work is complex and multifaceted, shaped by technological, social, and economic forces. As we navigate this evolving landscape, it's essential to embrace change, invest in people, and create opportunities for everyone to thrive. The future of work holds great promise, and by working together, we can build a more inclusive, resilient, and dynamic world of work.

8

Chapter 8: Sustainable Technology

Sustainable technology is becoming increasingly important as we face global challenges such as climate change, resource depletion, and environmental degradation. The development and adoption of sustainable technologies are crucial for creating a more resilient and environmentally friendly future. These technologies aim to minimize negative environmental impacts, promote resource efficiency, and support a transition to a low-carbon economy.

Renewable energy sources, such as solar, wind, and hydroelectric power, are at the forefront of sustainable technology. These energy sources generate electricity without emitting greenhouse gases, reducing our dependence on fossil fuels and mitigating climate change. Advances in renewable energy technologies, such as improved solar panels and more efficient wind turbines, are making clean energy more accessible and affordable.

Energy storage technologies, such as batteries and pumped hydro storage, play a critical role in the transition to renewable energy. These technologies enable the storage of excess energy generated by renewable sources, ensuring a stable and reliable supply of electricity. As energy storage technology continues to improve, it will enhance the viability of renewable energy and support the integration of distributed energy resources into the grid.

Sustainable transportation is another key area of focus. Electric vehicles (EVs) are gaining popularity as an alternative to traditional gasoline-powered cars. EVs produce zero tailpipe emissions, reducing air pollution and greenhouse gas emissions. Advances in battery technology are extending the range and affordability of EVs, making them a more attractive option for consumers. Additionally, innovations in public transportation, such as electric buses and high-speed rail, are contributing to more sustainable and efficient urban mobility.

Circular economy principles are transforming how we produce and consume goods. The circular economy aims to minimize waste and maximize the use of resources by designing products for longevity, reparability, and recyclability. This approach contrasts with the traditional linear economy, where products are made, used, and disposed of. By adopting circular economy practices, businesses can reduce their environmental footprint, create new value streams, and contribute to a more sustainable future.

Smart agriculture technologies are helping to address the challenges of feeding a growing global population while minimizing environmental impacts. Precision agriculture uses data and technology to optimize farming practices, improving crop yields and resource efficiency. Techniques such as drip irrigation, remote sensing, and autonomous farm machinery are reducing water usage, chemical inputs, and energy consumption. Sustainable farming practices, such as regenerative agriculture and agroforestry, are also gaining traction as ways to restore soil health and biodiversity.

Sustainable technology extends to buildings and infrastructure. Green building practices prioritize energy efficiency, water conservation, and the use of sustainable materials. Innovations such as passive solar design, green roofs, and smart building systems are

also becoming standard in many regions. These practices ensure that buildings not only reduce their environmental impact but also provide healthier and more comfortable living and working spaces.

Water conservation is another critical aspect of sustainable technology. Technologies like rainwater harvesting, greywater recycling, and desalination are helping to address the global water crisis. By efficiently managing water resources, we can reduce water scarcity and ensure a sustainable supply for future generations.

CHAPTER 8: SUSTAINABLE TECHNOLOGY

Sustainable technology also encompasses waste management. Innovations in recycling, waste-to-energy processes, and biodegradable materials are helping to reduce the amount of waste that ends up in landfills. Advanced recycling technologies can recover valuable materials from electronic waste, plastic, and other discarded products, creating a circular economy where resources are continuously reused.

As we continue to innovate and develop sustainable technologies, it's essential to consider the social and economic impacts of these advancements. Ensuring that sustainable technologies are accessible and affordable to all communities is crucial for creating a just and equitable transition to a low-carbon economy. Collaboration between governments, businesses, and civil society is necessary to drive the adoption of sustainable practices and technologies on a global scale.

The journey toward a sustainable future is challenging, but it holds immense promise. By embracing sustainable technology, we can create a world where economic growth and environmental stewardship go hand in hand. The choices we make today will shape the future of our planet and ensure that future generations can thrive in a healthy and resilient environment.

9

Chapter 9: Biotechnology and Health

Biotechnology is revolutionizing the field of health and medicine, offering new possibilities for diagnosis, treatment, and prevention of diseases. By harnessing the power of living organisms and biological systems, biotechnology is driving advancements that improve human health and well-being.

One of the most significant contributions of biotechnology is the development of new and more effective medical treatments. Biopharmaceuticals, such as monoclonal antibodies and gene therapies, are transforming the way we treat conditions like cancer, autoimmune diseases, and genetic disorders. These treatments target the underlying causes of diseases, offering more precise and personalized approaches to healthcare.

Genomics, the study of an individual's genes and their functions, has opened new avenues for personalized medicine. Advances in genomic sequencing technologies have made it possible to analyze a person's genetic makeup quickly and affordably. This information can be used to tailor treatments and preventive strategies based on an individual's unique genetic profile. Personalized medicine is moving us toward a future where healthcare is customized to the specific needs of each patient.

Biotechnology is also playing a crucial role in the development of vaccines and diagnostics. The rapid development of COVID-19 vaccines demonstrated the power of biotechnology to respond to global health crises. mRNA

CHAPTER 9: BIOTECHNOLOGY AND HEALTH

vaccine technology, used in some of the COVID-19 vaccines, represents a breakthrough in vaccine development, with potential applications for a wide range of infectious diseases. Diagnostic technologies, such as CRISPR-based tests, are enabling faster and more accurate detection of diseases, improving patient outcomes.

In addition to human health, biotechnology is addressing challenges in agriculture and food security. Genetically modified organisms (GMOs) and genome editing technologies, such as CRISPR-Cas9, are being used to develop crops with improved yield, resilience, and nutritional content. These advancements are helping to ensure a stable and sustainable food supply for a growing global population.

Biotechnology also holds promise for environmental sustainability. Bioengineering techniques are being used to develop biofuels, biodegradable materials, and bioremediation processes that can clean up environmental pollutants. These technologies offer solutions to some of the most pressing environmental challenges, contributing to a more sustainable and resilient future.

Despite its many benefits, biotechnology raises ethical and societal questions. The use of genetic information, the potential for designer babies, and the environmental impacts of GMOs are some of the concerns that need to be carefully considered. Ensuring that biotechnology is developed and applied responsibly requires collaboration between scientists, policymakers, and the public.

Biotechnology is transforming health and medicine, offering new possibilities for improving human well-being. As we continue to explore the potential of biotechnology, we must navigate its ethical and societal implications thoughtfully and responsibly. The future of biotechnology holds immense promise, and its impact on our lives and the world around us will be profound.

10

Chapter 10: The Role of Education

Education is a cornerstone of innovation and progress, shaping the minds and skills of future generations. As technology continues to evolve rapidly, the role of education in preparing individuals for the challenges and opportunities of the future is more critical than ever. Embracing new approaches to education and integrating technology into learning can create a more dynamic and effective educational system.

One of the most significant changes in education is the integration of digital technologies into the classroom. Online learning platforms, educational apps, and interactive digital tools are transforming how students learn and engage with content. These technologies offer personalized and adaptive learning experiences, catering to the individual needs and learning styles of students. By leveraging technology, educators can create more engaging and effective learning environments.

STEM education (Science, Technology, Engineering, and Mathematics) is becoming increasingly important in preparing students for the future workforce. As technology continues to shape various industries, a strong foundation in STEM subjects is essential for developing critical thinking, problem-solving, and analytical skills. Encouraging students to pursue STEM education and careers is crucial for fostering innovation and addressing global challenges.

Lifelong learning and continuous skill development are also vital in an era

CHAPTER 10: THE ROLE OF EDUCATION

of rapid technological change. As industries evolve and new technologies emerge, individuals must continually update their skills to remain competitive and relevant. Education systems must adapt to support lifelong learning, offering opportunities for reskilling and upskilling throughout a person's career. This approach ensures that individuals can navigate the changing job market and seize new opportunities.

Inclusivity and accessibility are essential considerations in modern education. Ensuring that all students, regardless of their background or abilities, have access to quality education is crucial for creating a more equitable society. Technology can play a significant role in achieving this goal by providing accessible learning materials, assistive technologies, and remote learning opportunities. Inclusive education fosters diversity and empowers individuals to reach their full potential.

Educators play a pivotal role in shaping the future of education. Supporting teachers with professional development, resources, and tools is essential for creating effective learning environments. Educators must also adapt to new teaching methods and technologies, embracing innovative approaches to instruction and assessment. Collaboration between educators, policymakers, and technology providers is necessary to create a supportive and dynamic educational ecosystem.

The role of education extends beyond academic learning to encompass social and emotional development. Schools are increasingly focusing on nurturing soft skills, such as communication, empathy, and teamwork, which are essential for success in the modern world. By fostering holistic development, education can prepare students to navigate the complexities of life and contribute positively to society.

Education is a powerful force for innovation and progress. As we embrace new technologies and approaches to learning, we must ensure that education systems are inclusive, adaptable, and forward-thinking. By investing in education and supporting lifelong learning, we can empower individuals to thrive in a rapidly changing world and drive the innovations that will shape our future.

11

Chapter 11: The Ethics of Innovation

As technology continues to advance at a rapid pace, the ethical considerations of innovation become increasingly important. The development and deployment of new technologies have far-reaching implications for society, raising questions about privacy, security, fairness, and accountability. Addressing these ethical challenges is essential for ensuring that innovation benefits everyone and aligns with our values and principles.

One of the primary ethical concerns in the digital age is privacy. The collection, storage, and use of personal data by technology companies have raised significant questions about how this information is protected and used. High-profile data breaches and scandals have underscored the need for robust data privacy regulations and transparent practices. Ensuring that individuals have control over their personal information and that data is used responsibly is crucial for building trust in technology.

Security is another critical ethical issue in the age of innovation. As we become more reliant on digital technologies, the risks of cyberattacks and security breaches increase. Protecting sensitive information, critical infrastructure, and digital systems from malicious actors is essential for maintaining trust and stability. Ethical considerations also extend to the development of cybersecurity technologies, ensuring that they are used for legitimate purposes and do not infringe on individual rights.

Fairness and bias in technology are significant ethical concerns, particularly in the context of artificial intelligence and machine learning. AI systems are often trained on large datasets, which can contain biases that are inadvertently incorporated into the algorithms. These biases can result in unfair treatment and discrimination in areas such as hiring, lending, and law enforcement. Addressing bias in AI requires diverse and representative datasets, transparent algorithms, and ongoing monitoring to ensure fairness and equity.

Accountability is essential for responsible innovation. As technologies become more complex and autonomous, determining responsibility for their actions and outcomes becomes challenging. Ensuring that developers, companies, and users are accountable for the ethical implications of technology is crucial for preventing harm and promoting responsible practices. Establishing clear guidelines and regulatory frameworks can help address accountability and ensure that technology is developed and used ethically.

The ethical considerations of innovation also extend to the societal impact of technology. Technological advancements can create significant social and economic changes, influencing employment, education, and access to resources. Ensuring that these changes are inclusive and equitable is essential for preventing disparities and promoting social justice. Policymakers, businesses, and civil society must work together to address the ethical implications of technology and create a future where innovation benefits all.

Innovation has the power to transform our world, but it must be guided by ethical principles and considerations. By addressing the ethical challenges of privacy, security, fairness, and accountability, we can ensure that technology is developed and deployed responsibly. The journey of ethical innovation requires collaboration, transparency, and a commitment to the values that define us as a society.

12

Chapter 12: Looking to the Future

As we look to the future, the pace of technological innovation shows no signs of slowing down. The advancements we have seen in recent decades are just the beginning, and the possibilities for future innovations are limitless. Embracing the potential of technology while addressing its challenges is essential to harness its potential for the greater good. The innovations of tomorrow will be driven by the collective efforts of scientists, engineers, entrepreneurs, and everyday individuals who dare to dream and push the boundaries of what's possible.

Emerging technologies such as quantum computing, nanotechnology, and synthetic biology hold the promise of revolutionizing our world in ways we can barely imagine. Quantum computing, for instance, has the potential to solve complex problems that are currently beyond the reach of classical computers. This technology could lead to breakthroughs in fields like cryptography, material science, and drug discovery, unlocking new possibilities for innovation and progress.

Nanotechnology, which involves manipulating matter at the atomic and molecular scale, offers exciting opportunities for advancements in medicine, electronics, and materials science. Nanomedicine, for example, could enable targeted drug delivery systems that treat diseases with unprecedented precision. Nanomaterials with unique properties could lead to the development of new electronic devices, stronger materials, and more efficient energy storage

CHAPTER 12: LOOKING TO THE FUTURE

solutions.

Synthetic biology, the design and construction of new biological parts and systems, is another frontier of innovation. This field has the potential to revolutionize healthcare, agriculture, and environmental sustainability. Synthetic biology could lead to the creation of custom organisms that produce biofuels, biodegradable plastics, and even new pharmaceuticals. The ability to engineer life at the molecular level holds immense promise for addressing some of the world's most pressing challenges.

As we look to the future, the importance of interdisciplinary collaboration and inclusive innovation cannot be overstated. The challenges we face are complex and interconnected, requiring diverse perspectives and expertise to develop effective solutions. By fostering a culture of collaboration and inclusivity, we can ensure that the benefits of innovation are shared by all and that no one is left behind.

Ethical considerations will continue to play a crucial role in guiding the development and deployment of new technologies. As we explore the frontiers of innovation, we must remain vigilant about the potential risks and unintended consequences. Ensuring that technology is developed and used responsibly, with a focus on human well-being and social justice, will be essential for creating a sustainable and equitable future.

The future of innovation is bright, filled with possibilities that have the potential to transform our world for the better. By embracing the spirit of curiosity, creativity, and collaboration, we can navigate the challenges ahead and unlock the full potential of technology. The journey of innovation is a continuous one, driven by our collective desire to explore, discover, and improve the world around us.

As we conclude this exploration of life in the fast lane of innovation, it's clear that the future holds immense promise. The technologies we develop today will shape the world of tomorrow, creating new opportunities and addressing the challenges we face. By harnessing the power of innovation, we can build a future that is sustainable, inclusive, and full of possibility.

description for the book "Tech Pulse: Life in the Fast Lane of Innovation":

In an era where technology shapes every facet of our lives, "Tech Pulse: Life in the Fast Lane of Innovation" delves into the exhilarating world of modern innovation. This insightful book takes you on a journey through the history and future of technological advancements, exploring how they have transformed our world and will continue to do so.

From the dawn of early inventions to the digital revolution, each chapter unravels the story of human ingenuity and its profound impact on society. Discover the rise of artificial intelligence, the Internet of Things, and the revolutionary potential of blockchain and cryptocurrencies. Learn how social media has reshaped communication, the evolving landscape of work, and the strides in sustainable technology that promise a greener future.

The book also tackles the ethical considerations of innovation, emphasizing the need for responsible and inclusive development. With a focus on biotechnology's contributions to health and the pivotal role of education, "Tech Pulse" provides a comprehensive overview of the forces driving our fast-paced technological world.

Packed with engaging narratives and thought-provoking insights, "Tech Pulse: Life in the Fast Lane of Innovation" is an essential read for anyone eager to understand the dynamic intersection of technology and human progress. Join us on this exciting ride through the ever-evolving landscape of innovation, and glimpse the limitless possibilities that lie ahead.

www.ingramcontent.com/pod-product-compliance
Lightning Source LLC
LaVergne TN
LVHW010444070526
838199LV00066B/6193